Native American Life

The Great Basin Indians

Daily Life in the 1700s

by Karen Bush Gibson

Consultant:
Troy Rollen Johnson, PhD
American Indian Studies
California State University
Long Beach, California

Capstone press

Mankato, Minnesota

Bridgestone Books are published by Capstone Press,
151 Good Counsel Drive, P.O. Box 669, Mankato, Minnesota 56002.
www.capstonepress.com

Library of Congress Cataloging-in-Publication Data
Gibson, Karen Bush.
    The Great Basin Indians: daily life in the 1700s / by Karen Bush Gibson.
    p. cm.—(Bridgestone books. Native American life)
    Summary: "A brief introduction to Native American tribes of the Great Basin, including their social
structure, homes, food, clothing, and traditions"—Provided by publisher.
    Includes bibliographical references and index.
    ISBN 0-7368-4318-3 (hardcover)
    1. Indians of North America—Great Basin—History—18th century—Juvenile literature. 2. Indians
of North America—Great Basin—Social life and customs—18th century—Juvenile literature. 3. Great
Basin—Antiquities—Juvenile literature. I. Title. II. Series.
E78.G67G53 2006
979.004'97—dc22   2005001634

Editorial Credits

Christine Peterson, editor; Jennifer Bergstrom, set designer; Ted Williams, book designer;
    Wanda Winch, photo researcher/photo editor; maps.com, map illustrator

Photo Credits

Corbis/Greg Probst, 20
Courtesy of Nevada State Museum, Carson City/Karen Beyers, cover, 10, 14, 18
McCormick Library of Special Collections, Northwestern University Library, 8
New York Public Library/Picture Collection, The Branch Libraries/Astor, Lenox, and
    Tilden Foundations, 12
Smithsonian American Art Museum/Gift of Marvin J. and Shirley F. Sonosky in memory of
    Harryette Cohn, 6
Used by permission, Utah State Historical Society, all rights reserved, 16

1 2 3 4 5 6 10 09 08 07 06 05

Table of Contents

Great Basin
Tribal Areas in the 1700s

Rocky Mountains

Paiute

Bannock

Shoshone

Washoe

Shoshone

Ute

Paiute

N
W   E
S

Scale
Miles
0   75   150   225   300

0   150   300
Kilometers

Legend

Mountain Range

The Great Basin and Its People

In the 1700s, Native Americans of the Great **Basin** depended on the land to live. The Great Basin covers parts of what is now the western United States. It looks like a giant bowl. **Tribes** have lived there for at least 12,000 years. Years ago, the Great Basin had many lakes. Some lakes dried up over time. The people **adapted** to desert life.

When European explorers arrived in the 1800s, the tribes were **thriving**. Everything in their daily life came from the land.

◀ Historic Great Basin tribal areas covered parts of what is today the west-central United States.

Social Structure

Most Great Basin Indians lived in small family groups. Some family groups formed **bands**. One or two families living together found it easier to find enough food. Men hunted, built homes, and made tools. Women cooked meals and made clothing.

Some bands joined together to form larger groups called tribes. Chiefs and councils led most tribes. These leaders decided when to hunt or go to war.

◄ Great Basin chiefs met in small camps to make decisions for their tribes.

Homes

Great Basin tribes had no permanent homes. People moved often to find food.

In summer, people lived in cooler mountain areas. Some tribes built wickiups from willow tree branches. Bark or grass covered these round homes. In cold weather, tribes added bark to make the walls thicker.

In winter, icy winds blew across the region. Tribes kept warm in canyons or caves. The Ute and Northern Shoshone lived in tepees made of wood frames covered with elk or buffalo hides.

◀ Wickiups made from tree branches and grass provided Great Basin tribes with shelter from the hot desert sun.

Food

Great Basin tribes moved often to gather and hunt for food. The rough land was not good for farming. People gathered seeds, roots, and grasses. They ate grasshoppers and other insects. In fall, tribes harvested **piñon**, or pine nuts. These nuts could be eaten alone or ground to make flour.

Men hunted and fished for food. Most tribes hunted rabbits and antelope. Some traveled great distances to hunt buffalo. The Washoe fished for salmon and trout. They dried extra meat for winter.

◄ Women filled baskets with nuts, roots, and grasses that they gathered across the Great Basin area.

Clothing

Native Americans of the Great Basin made their clothes from materials they got from the land. Women wove grasses and soft tree bark into skirts. Men wore **breechcloths** made from milkweed plants. Sandals of tule reeds or cattails protected feet from the hot desert sand.

In winter, people wore clothes made from animal hides. A cape of rabbit skins could also be used as a blanket. Each cape was made from at least 100 rabbit skins. Some bands made clothing from buffalo skins.

◀ Great Basin tribes wore dresses and pants made from a sturdy cloth woven from grasses.

Trading and Economy

The people of the Great Basin traded with people of the Southwest and Great Plains. Women of the Great Basin traded baskets for food. Great Basin hunters traded meat and animal skins. In return, they received knives, tools, blankets, and clothing.

By the early 1700s, tribes like the Ute and Shoshone traded with Spanish explorers for horses. Tribes could then travel farther to hunt buffalo. Daily life became easier.

◀ Great Basin hunters used long nets to trap rabbits. Tribes traded rabbit skins for goods from other tribes.

Leisure Time

In the 1700s, Great Basin tribes spent most of their time gathering food and supplies. In their free time, people enjoyed guessing games. Adults and children played Kill the Bone. One member of a team hid a bone. The other team guessed who had it.

During special celebrations, people had time for games. Races and ball games were popular. Many games prepared boys for hunting and war. Young men and women often met marriage partners during games between tribes.

◀ In this 1873 photograph, Paiute Indians play Kill the Bone just as it was played in the 1700s.

Traditions

In the Great Basin, Native Americans held **ceremonies** to celebrate the importance of food. Round Dances celebrated the piñon harvest. Many tribes held the Bear Dance in early spring. After four days of dancing and singing, the Ute and other tribes prayed for a good hunt.

Tribes used pipes in many ceremonies. Many tribes believed that holding a pipe protected that person from danger. Some pipes were made from green stone. Others were made of wood.

◄ Great Basin tribes celebrated harvest and other events by gathering for Round Dances.

Passing On Traditions

The Great Basin people used nature to share their history with others. In the 1700s, tribes did not have a written language. The Ute and other tribes carved pictures in desert rocks. These pictures told of hunts, battles, and other events.

Elders also told stories about the tribe's traditions. A spirit called Coyote was part of many stories. People believed that Coyote made the earth. Carvings and stories helped Great Basin tribes teach others about their past.

◀ Ute carvings in Arches National Park in Utah tell of a tribe's hunt from hundreds of years ago.

Glossary

adapt (uh-DAPT)—to change to fit into a new or different environment

band (BAND)—a group of Indian people who are related to each other; a band is smaller than a tribe.

basin (BAY-suhn)—a low area on the surface of the land

breechcloth (BREECH-kloth)—a short, skirtlike garment that is tied around the waist and has open slits on the sides

ceremony (SER-uh-moh-nee)—formal actions, words, or music performed to mark an important occasion

piñon (pin-YON)—pine nut from the cones of pine trees in the western United States

thrive (THRIVE)—to do well

tribe (TRIBE)—a group of people who share the same language and way of life

Read More

Ansary, Mir Tamim. *Great Basin Indians.* Native Americans. Des Plaines, Ill.: Heinemann, 2000.

Thoennes Keller, Kristin. *The Shoshone: Pine Nut Harvesters of the Great Basin.* America's First Peoples. Mankato, Minn.: Blue Earth Books, 2004.

Internet Sites

FactHound offers a safe, fun way to find Internet sites related to this book. All of the sites on FactHound have been researched by our staff.

Here's how:
1. Visit *www.facthound.com*
2. Type in this special code **0736843183** for age-appropriate sites. Or enter a search word related to this book for a more general search.
3. Click on the **Fetch It** button.

FactHound will fetch the best sites for you!

Index